MMO
3104A

Johann Sebastian
BACH

TWO CONCERTI
for VIOLIN *and* ORCHESTRA

CONTENTS

CONCERTO IN A MINOR
BWV1041
I. *(Allegro moderato)* 2
II. *Andante* 4
III. *Allegro assai* 5

CONCERTO IN E MAJOR
BWV1042
I. *Allegro* 8
II. *Adagio* 14
III. *Allegro assai* 15

To access audio visit:
www.halleonard.com/mylibrary

Enter Code
4012-4481-4962-6540

ISBN 978-1-59615-133-8

Music Minus One

EXCLUSIVELY DISTRIBUTED BY
Hal•Leonard®
7777 W. BLUEMOUND RD. P.O. BOX 13819 MILWAUKEE, WI 53213

Visit Hal Leonard Online at
www.halleonard.com

MMO 3104A

CONCERTO
for VIOLIN *and* ORCHESTRA
A MINOR ♃ A-MOLL
BWV1041

One measure of taps (two taps) precedes music

Johann Sebastian Bach
(1685-1750)

(Allegro moderato)

II.

III.

One measure of taps (three taps) precedes music

Allegro assai

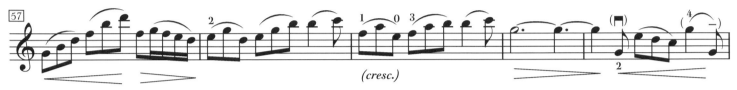

CONCERTO

for VIOLIN *and* ORCHESTRA

E MAJOR ♃ E-DUR

BWV1042

One measure of taps (4 taps) precedes music

Johann Sebastian Bach
(1685-1750)

II.

III.

One measure of taps (3 taps) precedes music

Allegro assai

Engraving: Wieslaw Novak